Writing Frames

Exmouth

PLEASE CHECK CD-ROM
IS INSIDE THE BACK COVER

review,

ent

Contents

First published 2002 by Folens Limited.
United Kingdom: Folens Publishers, Apex Business Centre, Boscombe Road, Dunstable, LU5 4RL.
Email: folens@folens.com

Ireland: Folens Publishers, Greenhills Road, Tallaght, Dublin 24.
Email: info@folens.ie

Poland: JUKA, ul. Renesansowa 38, Warsaw 01-905.

Editor: Alison MacTier
Layout artist: Patricia Hollingsworth
Cover design: Martin Cross
Illustrations: Tony O'Donnell – Graham-Cameron Illustration, Trevor Parkin – Linda Rogers Associates

© 2002 Folens Limited, on behalf of the authors.

Every effort has been made to trace the copyright holders of material used in this publication. If any copyright holder has been overlooked, we should be pleased to make any necessary arrangements.

British Library Cataloguing in Publication Data. A catalogue record for this publication is available from the British Library.

ISBN1 84303 111-6

Introduction

The series *English Writing Frames for Ages 11–14* provides structured support, detailed plans, and a wide range of ideas for teachers charged with ensuring students' skills in English are reviewed, developed and, where necessary, newly learned.

The structure of the units is common across the series, each unit consisting of four pages and sequenced in the following order.

Sheet 1: Teacher resource
This provides a highly structured lesson plan, featuring:

Main objectives – the main focus of the work, taken from the *Framework for Teaching English*

Additional focus – other skills or knowledge covered throughout the work

Starter activity – an initial task or tasks for the class, providing a focus for the work to come, reviewing skills covered previously, and so on

Further preparation – further tasks for the class or individual students, based on the resources provided

Main activity – guidance on how to use the writing frame provided

Maximising attainment – suggestions on how more confident or weaker students can be supported.

Sheet 2: Source material
Original sources from a range of writers, classical and modern, in a range of forms (poems, prose, screenplay, comic strip and so on). These may be used as overhead transparencies.

Sheet 3: Worksheet (or further source material)
Usually, a task aimed at preparing students for the main writing assignment. In some units, a different source text is provided where the focus demands it.

Sheet 4: Writing frame
In most cases, the writing frame brings together the skills covered throughout the unit, and provides an essential template around which students can 'hang' the ideas they have worked on.

Using the CD

There is a CD to accompany each title in the series. Each CD provides all the student resources with carefully adjusted tasks to suit on-screen work. Key features include:
- a facility for the teacher to *modify and adapt* the frames to suit his or her students
- a facility to *switch between screens*, and cut and paste key information or ideas between one screen and another
- a *'drop-down' menu of key vocabulary*, that students can access and place in their writing
- a *print out of the frames*, in which the boxes disappear, leaving only continuous prose or verse (the boxes also expand on screen so that students can add unlimited prose text, where appropriate)
- a facility to project text on to a screen or electronic whiteboard for demonstration and modelling work.

Analyse, review, comment consists of a wide range of source texts including a film review, a sports report and a storyboard, as well as formal commentary on a Shakespeare text. The teaching points address relevant objectives for Years 7 and 8 from *Text Level – Writing* in the *Framework for Teaching English*. There are cross-references on the contents page to these objectives, but teachers will see that many additional targets are also covered, too numerous to list here.

Identifying criteria and evaluating a text

Main Objective

- *To identify criteria for evaluating a particular situation ... present findings fairly and give a personal view.*

Additional Focus

- To compare and contrast story openings and *structure a story with an arresting opening.*

Starter Activity

- Ask students to think of different ways a story or film might begin (for example by presenting character, setting, action, or through dialogue). They should give specific examples.

Further Preparation

- This unit gives students the opportunity to contrast the different ways of opening a story and identifying the characteristics of successful ones. Students can also note that the same author might use different styles, since both the extracts on the source material sheet come from novels by Betsy Byars. Read these to the students, emphasising their contrasting tones and discuss briefly the general differences between the two. For example, the former is exciting; the latter, thoughtful. Clarify any American vocabulary, as needed.

  Give out the worksheet 'Looking at differences', page 6, and discuss the guidelines at the top of the sheet. Students should have no further help at this stage, but they should work in pairs to record a range of contrasting features in the two openings. When completed, ask them to report back, discuss their findings, and record the most pertinent comments. They should then consider why both openings are successful by identifying the features they have in common. Through discussion, help students to pinpoint the following: how they make the reader curious and want to read on; how they create an imaginative scene through character, setting, action and dialogue; how they appeal to a particular audience.

  Conclude by reminding students that a successful story opening is not merely one type (for example 'exciting').

Main Activity/ Using the Frame

- Once students have grasped the generalisations discussed above, along with any others you think important, they should complete the writing frame. They are asked to write about story openings in relation to children's literature and, before beginning, you may wish to discuss the opening of a book they are currently studying, so they can apply the criteria they have listed above and modify these if necessary. Encourage students to write paragraphs or developed sentences when completing the frame.

Maximising Attainment

- Students can study the source material further by looking at the importance of description in setting the scene. For example, they can compare the first paragraph in **A** with the following, which is a less successful paragraph: 'The dog ran out of the alley with a Cracker Jack box in his mouth. The boy followed quickly.'

  This work can be followed by giving students practice in writing openings from different perspectives. They can choose from these and develop a story.

Two story openings

Both these story openings come from different books, but they are written by the same author. Read each one carefully.

A

The pigeons flew out of the alley in one long swoop and settled on the awning of the grocery store. A dog ran out of the alley with a torn Cracker Jack box in his mouth. Then came the boy.

The boy was running hard and fast. He stopped at the sidewalk, looked both ways, saw that the street was deserted and kept going. The dog caught the boy's fear, and he started running with him.

The two of them ran together for a block. The dog's legs were so short he appeared to be on wheels. His Cracker Jack box was hitting the sidewalk. He kept glancing at the boy because he didn't know why they were running. The boy knew. He did not even notice the dog behind him or the trail of spilled Cracker Jacks behind.

From *The Eighteenth Emergency* by Betsy Byars

B

Sometimes at night when the rain is beating against the windows of my room, I think about that summer on the farm. It has been five years, but when I close my eyes I am once again by the creek watching the black fox come leaping over the green, green grass. She is as light and free as the wind, exactly as she was the first time I saw her.

Or sometimes it is that last terrible night, and I am standing beneath the oak tree with the rain beating against me. The lightning flashes, the world is turned white for a moment, and I see everything as it was – the broken lock, the empty cage, the small tracks disappearing into the rain. Then it seems to me that I can hear, as plainly as I heard it that August night, above the rain, beyond the years, the high, clear bark of the midnight fox.

From *The Midnight Fox* by Betsy Byars

███████████████████████

Looking at differences

1. What are the differences between the two story openings you have just heard? Think about:

- what is happening
- where the story takes place
- how many characters there are
- how the characters are feeling.

2. Write your answers in the table below and compare the differences.

Story openings

The Eighteenth Emergency	*The Midnight Fox*

Analyse, review, comment

Writing frame

There are many kinds of story openings. For example

There are also

But any good story opening for a children's book should have certain features.

First of all

Secondly

Thirdly

Of all these points I think the most important is

because

Identifying criteria and evaluating an object

Main Objective

- *To identify criteria for evaluating a particular ... object ... present findings fairly and give a personal view.*

Additional Focus

- *To collect, select and assemble ideas in a suitable planning format, e.g. star chart.*

Starter Activity

- Recap or explain how connectives help us to clarify our thinking. Give examples of those used for contrast and consequence, such as 'on the other hand', 'but', 'while', 'however' and 'so', 'therefore', 'consequently'. Ask students to think of instances in which they might be used. For example, 'I lost my money, so I could not get home'. Record the connectives to be referred to later.

Further Preparation

- The source material 'Annie's flip book', presents students with two examples of the same design product, the first unsuccessful, the second successful. (You may need to explain how a flip book works, although most students should know.) By contrasting the two, students can identify a series of suitable criteria more easily for evaluating a design. Discuss the examples with the class and ask students to contrast them, explaining any vocabulary as necessary. You may wish to draw up a two-column table to note findings such as: 'suitable fixer', 'unsuitable fixer'. In particular, as the class works through the contrasts, refer to the connectives in the starter activity to identify problems or achievements in the design. For example, when referring to **A**, we might say, 'The pages are not all the same size, so you would not be able to see the picture change.'

  Once the contrasts have been made, students should work alone or in pairs to complete the worksheet 'A good design', page 10. You may need to demonstrate how to use the star chart. Brief notes or questions can be added at the end of each arrow. For example: 'must work', 'will it work?' (Introduce the term *criteria* if you think suitable.)

Main Activity / Using the Frame

- Discuss students' findings, identifying a range of the most appropriate. Give out the writing frame and, referring to the starter activity once more, ask students to identify some of the opening connectives in the frame. They should now be sufficiently familiar with these to complete the work alone, giving a personal view and using their list of criteria.

Maximising Attainment

- Students can apply this technique to a range of examples, such as evaluating a plan or proposal, evaluating a character's actions and motivations in a novel, or assessing the ingredients of a good plot, opening or conclusion.

  Revise the usefulness of the conditional. Students may have used it when completing their writing frames (particularly 'would') to show that the flip book depended on certain features in order to work.

  Ask students to make a flip book at home and note any other criteria for a good design.

Annie's flip book

Annie's teacher asked her to design and make a flip book for homework, but she forgot. She remembered at the last minute. When she gave it to her teacher, she was asked to try again. So she made a second one. Below are the two flip books. Study the differences between them.

A

Materials
lined paper

Fixers
paperclip

Specifications
2cm x 4cm
number of pages: 10

Annie's first flip book

B

Materials
thin card

Fixers
glue

Specifications
7cm x 5cm
number of pages: 25

Annie's second flip book

A good design

Use Annie's flip book and the work you have already done to complete this star chart. Note down all the things you need to consider (criteria) for a good design.

Flip book

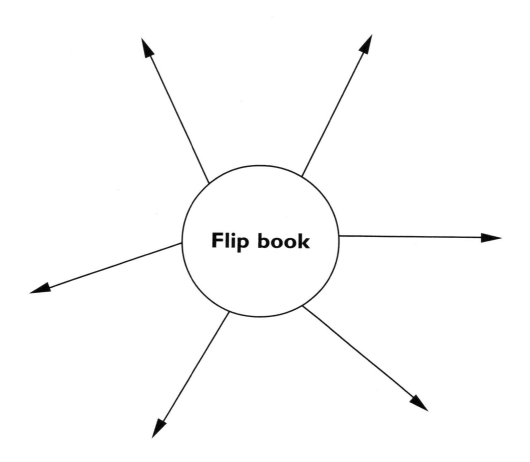

Analyse, review, comment

Writing frame

Write down your own view about the two flip books Annie made. Try to use *would* and *should* to say whether or not you think they would work.

I was asked to compare

The first was made from

So

It was also

Therefore

On the other hand, the second

In addition to this

Consequently

Identifying criteria and evaluating an event

Main Objective

⊙ *To identify criteria for evaluating a particular ... event, present findings fairly and give a personal view.*

Additional Focus

⊙ To expand sentences using connectives, phrases or clauses.

Starter Activity

⊙ News reports often contain lengthy sentences full of clauses and phrases, reflecting the speed with which the material is written. Give students a series of short sentences that can be linked into one sentence by phrases, pointing out the connectives. For example, 'Two girls narrowly escaped injury. The traffic lights failed in Felstead High Street. This happened last Saturday.' could read: 'Two girls narrowly escaped injury when the traffic lights failed *in* Felstead High Street *last* Saturday.' Record these on the board and explain that a connective is a word or series of linking words.

Further Preparation

⊙ Here, the source material, a fictitious newspaper report on a school event, can be used to help students evaluate the success of the event and also to examine ways in which extended sentences are written.

Read the local news report with students and discuss the gist of it. Focus on sentence length, helping students to see which words have been dropped from the three short sentences in question 1, to create the example given. Point to the main clause: 'Holly James, Sam Crosby and Jacob Mann were celebrating today', and the use of phrases as another way of combining sentences.

Students can then try to complete the remaining work alone or in pairs. Question 3 could be written: 'Next year the pupils hope to repeat their success *but this time* they plan to reach their target of £3000 *by* inviting a television celebrity to award the prizes.' Again students could work alone or in pairs to complete the worksheet, 'Seven good aims', page 14. They will need to have the news report available to identify the aims. The first has been completed for them. The remainder might include: to involve parents; to involve the wider community; to involve all members of the school; to learn organisational skills; to learn ICT skills; to learn team skills. They should number the aims in order of importance.

Main Activity/ Using the Frame

⊙ Ask students to report back and discuss their findings. Record their points. They should decide whether the summer fair met all the aims (or criteria) and what else is to be done in the future. Students can work alone to complete the writing frame, selecting from the aims discussed.

Maximising Attainment

⊙ Students can gain practice in extending a main clause by adding phrases such as: 'The old mill *next to the river* was flooded *with water and sludge.*'

They can try writing about an event in school or the community, evaluating its strengths and weaknesses and referring to 'Markfield makes a mark' as a model. Give students (or ask them to find) examples of local newspapers, tabloids and broadsheets and examine them for differences. They can, for example, compare a paragraph from each or look at the differences in layout.

Markfield makes a mark

1. Read the following extract from a local newspaper report:

> Holly James, Sam Crosby and Jacob Mann, three pupils from Markfield High School and the brains behind the summer fair, were celebrating today. The money they raised will go to the school's swimming pool fund, along with an additional grant from the Government, which has pledged support as a result of the young people's efforts.
>
> "The summer fair raised £2500, almost reaching our target of £3000," said Mr Jackson, the headteacher, adding, "We are delighted with the result. Everyone has put in a huge effort, but special praise goes to Holly, Sam and Jacob, who wanted to involve parents and the wider community as well as the whole school."
>
> The summer fair was not just about raising money. Pupils learned organisational skills, and how to use ICT to make posters and fliers. Teamwork was the key to their success.

Newspaper reports often have long sentences. These can be written as several shorter sentences but they would not sound like a newspaper report. For example, the first sentence could be written as three sentences.

- Holly James, Sam Crosby and Jacob Mann are three pupils from Markfield High School.
- They are the brains behind Markfield School's summer fair.
- They were celebrating today.

2. Write the second sentence as four shorter sentences.

_____

_____

_____

_____

3. Write a final sentence for the report by combining these into one:

- Next year the pupils hope to repeat their success.
- They plan to reach their target of £3000.
- They hope to invite a television celebrity to award the prizes.

_____

_____

_____

_____

Seven good aims

Before Markfield School's summer fair could be considered, the headteacher, Mr Jackson, said to the students, "What do you expect the fair to achieve? When you have seven good aims come back and see me!"

1. Use the newspaper report to decide what the pupils' aims were. The first has been done for you.

- *To reach the target of £3000*

-

-

-

-

-

-

2. Now number the points in order of importance.

Analyse, review, comment

Writing frame

Complete the frame below. Select aims from the work you have already done.

> *The students at Markfield School helped to run*

> *Their main aim was to*

> *However, they also had other aims. For example*
>
> *and also*

> *In my view the summer fair was a success because*
>
> *but*

Games review

Main Objective

○ *To write reflectively about a text, taking account of the needs of others who might read it.*

Additional Focus

○ To identify and interpret language play (for example, play on words, metaphor).

Starter Activity

○ Carry out a brainstorming activity on current computer games, asking students to categorise them loosely into popular and unpopular groups. Help them identify one or two important features for a successful game.

Further Preparation

○ Discuss the chatty tone and language used on the source material sheet so that the students understand the gist of the review (which, typically, is also written in the present tense). Metaphor, rather than jargon, is used, since some students will not be familiar with the latter. (For example, the play on 'whiskers' refers to cat's whiskers being tame, werewolf's 'whiskers' or beard being wild and the object of the game is to avoid becoming a werewolf, as well as transforming the werewolf of the game into a cat.)

Many students will be familiar with a range of computer games and may even be aficionados. Since students often hold strong views about such games, it can be difficult to write objectively or reflectively. By asking them to choose a game they either like or hate, they can express a bias, while still attempting to be objective. This should make the tasks of completing the worksheet 'Game plan', page 18, and writing a review accessible.

Main Activity/ Using the Frame

○ Here, students should bring their reading and planning to bear and use the source material 'Werewolf' as a model. Most importantly, they should write several sentences under each paragraph, using the 'useful words' at the bottom of the page along with the good and bad points they have already assembled. (Please note, 'useful words' are listed roughly in chronological order to help students structure their reviews.) Some students may wish to introduce jargon into their reviews and should be encouraged to do so.

Maximising Attainment

○ It is best if students present their work to each other in small groups rather than to the class as a whole, unless they are especially confident. If the focus of the discussion in the group is the game being reviewed, a range of other perspectives can be noted. For example, it may be that one student in the group is especially interested in graphics and can add comments.

The students can record these additional comments by annotating their texts briefly, in the light of the discussion. Once the discussion is completed, students can consider how and where they might include further sentences to cover the points. This requires some skill and they should be selective, adding one or two sentences only to their basic text. They can then redraft their work and keep it for reference.

Where possible, discuss and ask students to explain the jargon used. This can lead to a discussion of what jargon is and how it is used both creatively and as a means of exclusion.

Werewolf

1. Read the following games review.

They seem to be all the fashion. There's hardly a game around these days that doesn't have a werewolf, though some are more like pussycat's whiskers. Not this one. This game with the name shows its teeth and will keep you running.

The object is to transform the werewolf into a lazy lap-cat (by finding a jewelled collar) and also avoid growing whiskers yourself. The sound effects are good too. Lots of howling at the moon and yelps when you get caught (and get caught you will). Even my fourteen-year-old daughter, who's a grand master, couldn't escape the treacherous terrain. The tricks are challenging. There are several kung-fu-type leaps that mean you take different directions through different landscapes: woods, mountains, deserts, cities and lots of others. One false leap and you've had it. You even have to keep your head above water after being thrown into a lake.

But there are drawbacks. First is the price tag. Secondly, when you've battled through, you won't want to play the game again. You'll just sit back and sigh with relief or collapse in a nervous heap. But for serious players, it's worth it.

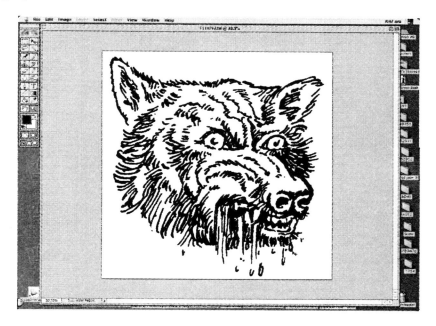

2. Underline three verbs in the first paragraph that tell you what tense the review is written in.

3. Underline the following in paragraphs 1 and 2. What do they mean or refer to? Write a short answer. The first has been done for you.

Phrase	Meaning
'pussycat's whiskers' 'this game with the name' 'shows its teeth' 'avoid growing whiskers yourself' 'treacherous terrain'	*not very difficult*

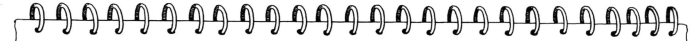

Game plan

1. Write down the title of a game you especially like or hate.

2. Try to list both the good and bad points of the game, not just one or the other.
Think about whether or not the game:

- is a real challenge
- makes you laugh
- has an interesting story
- has interesting characters
- keeps your attention.

Good points   **Bad points**

Writing frame

1. Review a game to present to other members of your class. Use the plan below and some of the key words at the bottom of the page. Think of your own, too.

Introduction (*write three or four sentences*)

Main comment (*what the game is about and whether you like it or not, and why*)

Extra comments and summing up (*write three or four sentences*)

Useful words

First	Secondly	I came across a particular game recently
My all-time favourite	If there's one game I can't stand	The object of the game
In addition	However	On the whole Finally

     Analyse, review, comment

Film review

Main Objective

- *To write reflectively about a text, taking account of the needs of others who might read it.*

Additional Focus

- Making notes.

Starter Activity

- Discuss with students the main differences between a film and book, such as the nature of the audience, audience involvement, the moving image, sound effects and the use of the imagination. Make the point, however, that a text can be taken to mean 'media text' as well as its more common usage.

Further Preparation

- The focus in this unit is on evaluating the students' own reviews in the light of discussion and peer group response, after studying a film review that can be used as a model.

  On the source material sheet, point to the title, noting the certificate and director. Read through the review with students, clarifying terms such as 'direction', 'casting' and 'music score'. Then work through the structure of the review. For example, ask students what the first paragraph is about (it opens with comments on plot and characters without retelling the story). Also help students to formulate useful questions. For example, in the second paragraph, which discusses direction and performances, the following questions might be asked: 'Were the performances successful?', 'If so, how?' The questions should be recorded as a checklist for future use. Also consider comparative links such as 'whilst', 'unfortunately' etc.

  Students should write their own reviews, alone or in pairs, on a film of their own choice, using 'The last days of summer' as a model and taking into account the structure and questions listed in discussion.

  Using the worksheet 'Reviewing my review', page 22, students should work in small groups or pairs to evaluate each other's reviews. As they discuss these in turn, each student can comment on their own reviews by ticking in the boxes provided, noting strengths and weaknesses. (This method still allows them to engage in discussion.) They can add a main target at the end under further comments, which can be discussed with you subsequently. Clearly, discussion needs to be carried out sensitively. Positive comments should be made and students might, for example, offer criticism of their own reviews before others do. Students can report back and the most useful, general points can be recorded.

Main Activity/ Using the Frame

- The purpose of the frame here is to help students evaluate their own reviews after discussion with others. The early prompts help them to identify the positive aspects of their work and the later prompts encourage them to reflect on how it can be improved. From this, students can isolate some targets for their next reviews.

Maximising Attainment

- Students can reflect on their group discussions and the value and difficulties encountered in reviewing each other's work, noting how to carry this out effectively. A 'positive discussion' checklist can be drawn up, detailing the most useful procedures.

  Students can collect a range of film reviews from magazines and newspapers, identifying common terminology. They can also write critical reviews of books that have been made into films, deciding what has been gained or lost from the original.

The last days of summer

The last days of summer (U) Morgan Spence 2001

This thoughtful tale, set during a flood in a small village near the Cornish coast, is sensitively depicted. The hero, Angelo (Gabriel Osti) is a young Italian boy who is spending the summer with his English aunt (Anna Marina). His experiences during the flood lead him to a better understanding of his family at home. The main theme is about growing up.

Morgan Spence guides the actors gently and has an eye for detail. The casting is excellent. Both Osti and Marina play their parts to perfection, as do the minor characters. Especially good is Jack Edley as a one-time Cornish fisherman having to find new work. The acting and direction throughout the film cannot be faulted.

The music score unfortunately does not quite fit the subject matter. At the height of the flood, a more dramatic score is required, whilst the film's quieter moments lend themselves to a softer one. The camerawork fares better. There are some wonderful aerial shots of the coastline and also an excellent close-up during the final surprise sequence.

Suitable for a family audience.

MG

Reviewing my review

As you discuss your review, tick one box in each line.
If you did not mention a point in your review, leave the boxes blank.

	Could be better	Quite good	Good	Very good
plot (without retelling the story)	☐	☐	☐	☐
characters	☐	☐	☐	☐
setting	☐	☐	☐	☐
theme	☐	☐	☐	☐
direction	☐	☐	☐	☐
performances	☐	☐	☐	☐
camerawork	☐	☐	☐	☐
music score	☐	☐	☐	☐
suitable audience	☐	☐	☐	☐

Further comments
What do you want to improve most? How can I do this?

Analyse, review, comment

Writing frame

I wrote a film review of

directed by

My most successful comments were about

and also

However, I could have added

and also

I agreed/did not agree with all of the comments made. In particular, I thought

Most of all I want to improve

To do this I will need to

A balanced view: a sports report

Main Objective

○ *To weigh different viewpoints and present a balanced analysis of an event.*

Additional Focus

○ To identify connectives, sporting language and style.

Starter Activity

○ Discuss a recent sports event with students, encouraging them to take a balanced view. This could be an event at a school sports day, a school fixture, swimming gala or a national event. Identify and list the main points for students to refer to, if needed. Ask them to provide suitable headlines and list these too.

Further Preparation

○ Sports reports can be written as recounts using mainly the past tense, although others are predictive and use the future and conditional. Some are written in chronological order. Others discuss biographical details of players, teams or clubs. Most have pace and all use sporting terms. The source material mock sports report, 'An oliphant never forgets', page 25, depicts a game in which one team is clearly better than the other, but the report attempts to present a balanced account. These attempts at balance deliberately stand out and students should be able to identify them in the fourth and final sentences, without help. The language used is demanding but the account is short and should be within students' capabilities, if discussed first. Note, in particular, how *jargon*, *colloquialism* and heightened or aggressive, language is used.

Discuss the play on words (a common feature of tabloid headlines) in the title 'oliphant' ('elephant'). You may also need to explain the use of 'former' and 'latter'.

The worksheet 'Long or short', page 26, draws attention to the other main features of sports reports – pace – conveyed through lengthy sentences with limited punctuation, and also truncated sentences.

Depending on the students' progress, you may wish to discuss these before the tasks on the sheet are attempted. (For example, if students are not aware of the function of connectives.)

Main Activity/ Using the Frame

○ The frame gives a clear structure for students to write three paragraphs: beginning, middle and end. These can be altered to suit the students' needs and the 'useful expressions' provided could also be added to. Students who are unfamiliar with sport can refer to the points already listed during the starter activity and base their report on these.

Maximising Attainment

○ You can use the sports report to point up the use of the past tense in recounts. Students can identify the verbs.

Students can also try writing a more sophisticated report using 'An oliphant never forgets' as a model.

Knowledgeable students can attempt to predict the outcome of a sports event and write a short report in the future and conditional tenses.

An oliphant never forgets

An oliphant never forgets

Lisport 4 Wexend 0
Byron Cardew

Wexend took a pasting in last Saturday's quarter-final as Lisport's ace striker, Gabriel Oliphant, scored a superb series of goals in a 4–0 home game at Lisport Bridge. A flare-up in the first-half between midfielders, Binny and Godley, led to the former being sent off. Wexend never recovered. However, Rixham, Doley and Potts struggled gallantly and showed that Wexend may still be a team to be reckoned with.

Opposition fans piled on the pressure. Despite fierce abuse, Gabes took it all in his stride, blowing a kiss to the terraces in the second half to show who was in charge. The Lisport faithful went wild as the striker secured a final header during the last minute of the match.

Oliphant has suffered mercilessly under Wexend taunts for some time.

"This boy doesn't forget. It brings an edge to his game and makes him a fierce opponent. He's the business," said elated coach, Dixon Grant.

"I'm gutted," wept one Wexend fan. "It's humiliation," but added nobly, "You've got to hand it to Oliphant. He's up there with the greats."

1. Why is the title of the sports report a play on words?

2. Each paragraph has a main point. Sum up what that is. For example, the first paragraph runs quickly through the match.

3. Lisport is clearly a better team than Wexend. Underline two sentences that show Byron Cardew has chosen information to give a balanced account.

4. What do these expressions mean?

   'took a pasting'   'flare-up'   'piled on the pressure'   'Lisport faithful'

   'suffered mercilessly under Wexend taunts'   'It's humiliation'

5. Why do you think aggressive language is often used in sports reports?

Long or short

1. Sports reports have a special style. They often have long sentences with lots of information. These sentences use connectives (link words) such as 'and', 'but', 'during', 'on the whole', 'rather than'.

2. Read these sentences again. Underline all the link words. The first has been done for you.

> Wexend took a pasting <u>in</u> last Saturday's quarter-final as Lisport's ace striker, Gabriel Oliphant, scored a superb series of goals in a 4–0 home game at Lisport Bridge. A flare-up in the first-half between midfielders Binny and Godley led to the former being sent off.

3. Sports reports also use short, sharp sentences.

'Wexend never recovered' really means *'Wexend never recovered from Binny being sent off.'*

4. Write down long versions of these sporting sentences.

- The team took a hammering. _____

- The pitch was cleared. _____

- The centre-back will be out for another week. _____

- A late decision is expected. _____

Analyse, review, comment

Writing frame

Use the frame below to write your own sports report. (It does not have to be about football.) Make it a balanced account. Write three paragraphs. Give your report a headline.

The result of

Despite

During

However

On the whole

Useful words and expressions

found a way to overcome	showed determination	kept his/her head
played confidently	took a drubbing	ruled out	tough enough
chance of victory	disaster loomed	took a tumble	rough ride

A balanced view:
an environmental issue

Main Objective

- *To weigh different viewpoints and present a balanced analysis of an issue* (for example, tourism).

Additional Focus

- To identify and use a range of connectives, such as sequential, logical, causal.

Starter Activity

- Discuss holidays students have been on, encouraging them to consider the kinds of holiday facilities available to them, the range of attitudes presented to visitors by local residents and the ways in which holidaymakers affect the environment.

Further Preparation

- The source material sheet, 'Tourism', looks at both the advantages and disadvantages of tourism, the principal advantages being the labour-intensive nature of this service industry and the idea of leisure. (The problems related to particular jobs such as catering and seasonal work are not discussed here, but you may wish to do so, particularly if students live in a tourist area.) Discuss each comment with students, asking them to separate out the advantages and disadvantages as they go. A table can then be drawn up and completed independently.

  Discuss or remind students how particular connectives can assist different kinds of thinking. For example, connectives such as, 'and', 'also', 'in addition', help sequencing; 'consequently', 'as a result', 'therefore', help logical and causal relationships to be made; 'on the other hand', 'however', helps another perspective to be expressed. The worksheet 'Making connections', page 30, focuses on the connectives that link more sophisticated ideas, since students have to take into account one view against another. Once discussion has taken place, they can carry out the task on their own or in pairs and report back. The following connectives are included: 'so', 'however', 'since', 'from', 'on the other hand', 'because', 'but', 'the outcome', 'consequently', 'although', 'as a result', 'now', 'nevertheless'.

Main Activity/ Using the Frame

- By the time students come to use the frame, they should be familiar with both the advantages and disadvantages of tourism and how to use a range of connectives. They will need to select information from the work already done, however, to complete the frame, which requires two paragraphs of several sentences. Those that need greater assistance can, with help, build a frame from the connectives provided on the sheet so that each sentence has a prompt but, as far as possible, students should try to do the work alone.

Maximising Attainment

- Students could continue the theme and look at solutions to the problems of tourism, such as regeneration through caring for the environment, ecotourism and sustainability and gain practice in using common connectives to present a range of viewpoints.

Tourism

1. Read what these people say about tourism. Most have more than one point of view.

A.
> I own a souvenir shop and my daughter runs a restaurant so we like tourists. However, our local tax and water bills are high, since the cost of cleaning the beaches is high.

B.
> I make money from renting out cottages in the summer. On the other hand, as a farmer, I don't like holidaymakers because some trample my fields and leave litter.

C.
> I run a small hotel, so I need guests, but last year the beaches were very dirty. The outcome was that we had fewer visitors.

D.
> House prices in our village have been pushed up because some people have holiday homes. Consequently, we can't afford to buy a house.

E.
> I love water sports and often visit the coast, although pollution can be a problem. As a result, I caught an ear infection.

F.
> The coastline used to be quiet years ago, with a range of wildlife. Now there are bars and clubs along the beach. Nevertheless, my job as a travel agent depends on tourists.

2. Make a list of the good points and bad points about tourism. Put your points in a table like this.

Advantages of tourism	Disadvantages of tourism

Making connections

1. Here are the comments people made on the resource sheet 'Tourism'.

2. Underline all the linking words (connectives) that help the people to connect the *main* ideas. Sometimes they help to connect a statement with a reason. Sometimes they help to show another point of view or connect the past and the present. (Don't, for example, highlight 'and', which only connects one thing after another.)

   The first has been done for you.

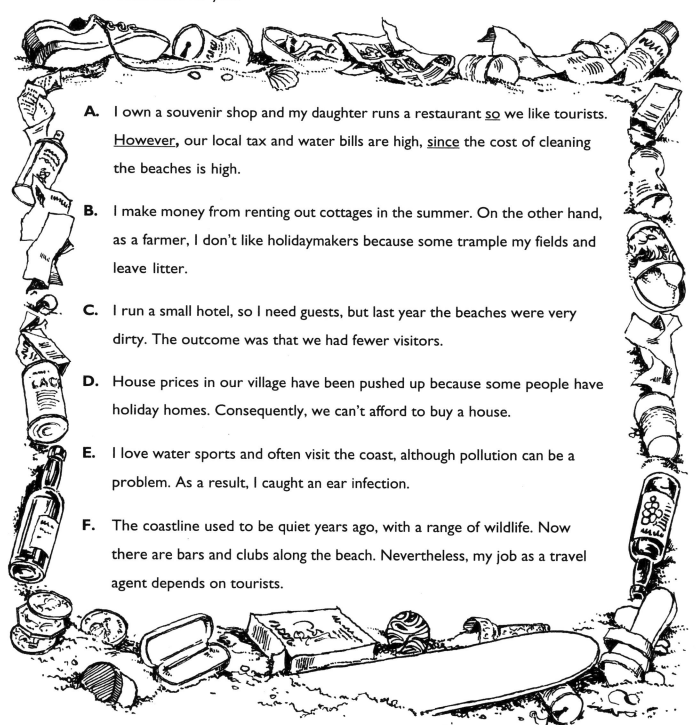

A. I own a souvenir shop and my daughter runs a restaurant <u>so</u> we like tourists. <u>However,</u> our local tax and water bills are high, <u>since</u> the cost of cleaning the beaches is high.

B. I make money from renting out cottages in the summer. On the other hand, as a farmer, I don't like holidaymakers because some trample my fields and leave litter.

C. I run a small hotel, so I need guests, but last year the beaches were very dirty. The outcome was that we had fewer visitors.

D. House prices in our village have been pushed up because some people have holiday homes. Consequently, we can't afford to buy a house.

E. I love water sports and often visit the coast, although pollution can be a problem. As a result, I caught an ear infection.

F. The coastline used to be quiet years ago, with a range of wildlife. Now there are bars and clubs along the beach. Nevertheless, my job as a travel agent depends on tourists.

Analyse, review, comment

Writing frame

1. Using what you have learned about tourism, choose information to write two paragraphs. The first one should be about the advantages of tourism, giving examples and reasons.

2. The second should be about the disadvantages. Again give examples and reasons. Use different kinds of connectives to link your ideas.

Tourism

On the other hand

Useful connectives

so	while	since	from	on the other hand	because	but
consequently	as well as		although	now		nevertheless
and also	in addition		the outcome	as a result		however

Analysing and evaluating a process

Main Objective

- ◉ *To integrate evidence into writing to support analysis or conclusions.*

Additional Focus

- ◉ To evaluate a process or product in relation to agreed criteria.
- ◉ To evaluate what has been learned about animation.

Starter Activity

- ◉ In this unit, students are asked to evaluate the presentation and content of the process involved in making an animation film and also what new information they have learned about how the film is created. In doing so, they will have to draw on evidence and arrive at conclusions. Begin by giving students brief information about how animation works, but do not explain the process in detail. You can, for instance, point out that it is a series of stills that are shot quickly in succession, rather like a flick book, which gives the impression of movement. Some animation uses flat images. Others use three-dimensional models.

Further Preparation

- ◉ Discuss the terms *criteria* and *evaluation*. Students should work in pairs to complete each box on the worksheet, 'Our criteria', page 34. However, before studying the source material, 'From storyboard to final shoot', ask them to consider what features make the presentation of a process they are familiar with successful (say of the digestive system or breathing). They should think about the use of diagrams and illustrations, headings, labels and so on, as well as content and language. They can write the criteria in the form of questions. This should help them to think coherently and explore ideas more easily. For example, in box **A** they might write, 'Is each stage clearly presented?' In box **B**, 'Can I understand the process?' Students should write at least four criteria in each box. Ask them to report back. Discuss the criteria they have used, recording on the board those both you and they think are the most appropriate.

  Working in the same pairs, students should study 'From storyboard to final shoot', apply the list of agreed criteria and decide whether or not the process meets these. In order to do this, they will need to draw on evidence. If it is successful, students should be able to deduce the meaning of the vocabulary used. (A question in relation to this could be asked under 'Our criteria'.)

Main Activity/ Using the Frame

- ◉ Discuss the students' outcomes and ask them to arrive at conclusions – for example, to consider any ways in which 'From storyboard to final shoot' could be improved. (For example, by the use of arrows or subheadings, fewer words, more stages.) Working alone, students should complete either or both writing frames according to their ability and the time available. (One could be given as a homework task.) They can copy out the frames as they write, allowing room for expansion. For example, in frame **A**, 'because' can prompt several comments. Students can add 'and also'.

Maximising Attainment

- ◉ Students can review the class list of criteria in the light of the work they have done and make changes as necessary. Ask them to underline the starter connectives, 'First', 'Next', 'Then', 'The final' in 'From storyboard to final shoot'. They can use these and others to create their own writing frames as supports when sequencing a process of events. They can evaluate a design product they have made in technology or at home. They will need to consider what materials and equipment were used and whether the product is functional.

  Students can also use storyboards to create their own plots.

From storyboard to final shoot

1. First, the artist creates characters and a storyboard of key frames in the film. These frames show how the characters will need to move.

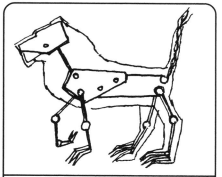

2. Next, a drawing is made of each character's armature.

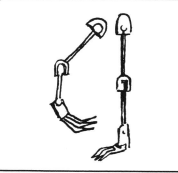

3. This is made using ball and socket joints, so the character will move.

4. A clay model is built around the armature and the model is painted.

5. Then the characters and their movements are filmed following the storyboard. The dialogue is added and the run-through is checked.

6. The animators shape the characters' mouths to match the dialogue, so it looks as if they are talking.

7. The final shoot is made. This can take months or even years, depending on the length of the film. For each second of filming, twenty-four frames are made!

Our criteria

1. Use this to evaluate how a process should be set out (such as how we breathe).

A. Presentation

List the questions you would ask to judge presentation.

1.

2.

3.

4.

B. Written information

List the questions you would ask to judge the written information.

1.

2.

3.

4.

Analyse, review, comment

Writing frame

The first frame is to help you evaluate how animation was explained. Make sure you include 'evidence' in your answers. The second is to help you analyse what you have learned about animation.

A Evaluation

I have been looking at the explanation of

On the whole, I thought that the way it was presented was

because

I thought that the written information was

But/ And I would also like to add that

B What I learned about animation

I have learned several things about

The most important thing I learned was

I also learned

I would like to learn more about

Critical review for older readers

Main Objective

- *Write a critical review of a substantial text, taking account of the context in which it was written and the likely impact on its intended readers.*

Additional Focus

- To identify and use the features of reviews which are appropriate for different readers, for example peers.
- To use a range of tenses effectively.

Starter Activity

- Although all students will automatically use a variety of complex tenses in everyday speech, those who experience learning difficulties are less likely to do so in writing effectively and are less aware of stylistic conventions. This starter activity looks at simple tenses used in reviews, building on work done in the previous unit. Recap the present tense, giving examples within the context of a review and a discussion of a character. Students can give further examples, referring to the current novel or story they are reading. Ensure they understand that we write reviews largely in the present tense. However, when we wish to reflect back about experience, we introduce the past tense, when we are projecting ourselves or others into the future, we use the future tense and when we wish to consider or recommend, we can use the conditional. Point out that these techniques give variety and interest to the writing. Record examples and discuss terminology.

Further Preparation

- Ask a student to read the source material, 'Reckless' and discuss what the story is about, clarifying any vocabulary as necessary. Discuss each paragraph with students, who should annotate the text by making brief notes at the end of each arrow. The review deals with a range of features: *character, setting and plot, style and structure, themes, criticism, recommendations.*

  Refer to the starter activity when giving out the worksheet 'Different tenses', page 38. Working alone or in pairs, students should identify examples of present, past, future and conditional. Remind them of the purpose of the tenses, also noting that they add variety to the writing. Avoid discussion of more complex tenses and terminology.

Main Activity/ Using the Frame

- Now refer to the sheet, 'Making a writing frame', pointing to the support cues and connectives at the bottom of the page. Discuss these in the context of a novel or short story students have studied. They should try to construct their own writing frame. They could work in pairs, but should write the review by themselves. Students can then change the frame as they write, inserting or modifying cues. Encourage them to develop their paragraphs.

Maximising Attainment

- With practice, students can learn to vary the writing style of their reviews, for example by beginning with a comment on setting or by changing tenses and using asides. (For example, if they wished to add an aside while commenting on an event in a novel, they might insert brackets and change tense ('a part of the story *I found* very true to life').)

Reckless by Dina Dale

1. When you have read and discussed the review, write notes at the end of the arrows to say what each paragraph is about.

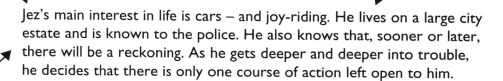

Jez's main interest in life is cars – and joy-riding. He lives on a large city estate and is known to the police. He also knows that, sooner or later, there will be a reckoning. As he gets deeper and deeper into trouble, he decides that there is only one course of action left open to him.

This gripping tale succeeds because the character of Jez is well developed. (Most other characters fade into the background and could have been written more interestingly.) The book is also rather short. However, the story has pace and suspense. The events take place during one summer and we are never quite sure how things will turn out for Jez.

In addition, the story deals with several issues to do with the way young people are treated and the way they regard others. There are few positive role models for Jez and little to do on the estate.

On the whole, I found this novel enjoyable. It should appeal to most teenagers who will be able to understand why Jez becomes involved in crime and what he needs to overcome his difficulties.

Dean Wilson

Different tenses

1. What *tense* is the review mainly written in? Find an example in each paragraph.
2. Find an example of each of the following: past tense, future tense, conditional tense.

Underline the examples and make notes, using arrows, to say what they are.

Reckless by Dina Dale

Jez's main interest in life is cars – and joy-riding. He lives on a large city estate and is known to the police. He also knows that, sooner or later, there will be a reckoning. As he gets deeper and deeper into trouble, he decides that there is only one course of action left open to him.

This gripping tale succeeds because the character of Jez is well developed. (Most other characters fade into the background and could have been written more interestingly.) The book is also rather short. However, the story has pace and suspense. The events take place during one summer and we are never quite sure how things will turn out for Jez.

In addition, the story deals with several issues to do with the way young people are treated and the way they regard others. There are few positive role models for Jez and little to do on the estate.

On the whole, I found this novel enjoyable. It should appeal to most teenagers who will be able to understand why Jez becomes involved in crime and what he needs to overcome his difficulties.

Dean Wilson

Making a writing frame

1. Choose a novel you have read to write a review for others in your class.
2. The writing frame below, which is to help you write a review, has been started. Complete it, using some of the examples at the bottom of the page to help you. Think of your own cues as well.

In (write name of novel) _____ *by (write name of author)*

_____ *the main character* _____

Useful cues and connectives

I found	On the whole	Consequently	I felt	I thought
However	While	I enjoyed	Readers should/would	
Some/You will	Finally	Although		

Analyse, review, comment   **39**

Formal and informal analysis I

Personal Commentary

- This unit should be used in conjunction with the next, which looks at formal analysis. The two can then be compared.

Main Objective

- *To explore and use different degrees of formality in written and oral texts.*

Additional Focus

- To identify the writer/reader relationship; to look at formal analysis and personal commentary.

Starter Activity

- You can begin by carrying out a brainstorming activity. Ask students to give examples of informal types of writing (such as postcards, personal letters, email, fridge notes and so on). Also ask them to explain what a *personal commentary* is, using the examples given. Emphasise that all of them feel close to the reader – as if the writer were there, speaking to them. Introduce the term *informal.*

Further Preparation

- The source material 'Working with the web' has several characteristics typical of personal commentary. It is non-chronological, uses the present tense, uses a rhetorical device, is evaluative and reflective and also has a close writer/reader relationship. The last of these is the main focus here and students are asked to look at the way in which punctuation and informal language create effects. Read the text with the students. Discuss what it is about and ask them to describe how the writer is speaking to them. Point to the way in which the writer uses casual language to address the reader and punctuation that positions the reader through asides, such as the use of brackets in the first paragraph. Since expression is important in understanding, you may need to re-read the text to students, stressing the asides.

  Show the students the examples in the worksheet 'Talking to the reader', page 42. They can work in pairs to complete the boxes.

Main Activity/ Using the Frame

- Ask students to report back. The following are examples that could be included. *Informal language:* paragraph 2, 'it's surprising'; paragraph 3, 'hit the roof'; paragraph 4, 'whichever way you look at it'. *Punctuation:* paragraph 2, the dash; paragraph 3, brackets and exclamation mark; paragraph 4, the question mark.

  The frame can be used to write a personal commentary about the same issue or another area of interest. Students should try to use the work they have done, particularly the use of punctuation to create asides.

Maximising Attainment

- Use the main text to discuss any of the following: the use of the present tense; the expression of a point of view; the use of jargon in specialist areas; various ways of opening and concluding informally – skills students often find difficult.

  Students can write informal letters to each other, expressing a personal point of view, for example about an environmental issue. They can also write such letters to magazines. Recap how an informal letter is set out, if necessary.

  Presenting a personal opinion to the class is also useful for developing speaking skills. Students can work in pairs to decide how to adapt their commentaries, for example by skimming for the main points and making three or four brief notes to memorise as cues.

Working with the web

Like many of my friends, I enjoy using the Internet and know my way around. I use it more than anyone at home, except perhaps my older sister, who likes anything interactive. My mum and dad use it occasionally, when they want to find something specific (but they're not very skilful – well, they don't play around with it the way we do).

There are many sites you can visit. Music sites must be one of the most popular. They're a favourite with my twin brother, who downloads regularly. I use the chat sites quite often, mainly through Internet Service Providers, but I sometimes use other routes too. I get in touch with other people my own age – it's surprising how much you have in common. You can swap ideas and discuss pop, fashion, whatever you like.

There are also other useful sites, such as educational ones. They're handy if you need to find out information for a project at school. If you just want to while away the hours, you can go to games sites, which can become a habit. That can be a problem (as my mum keeps telling me!) because you can spend too long in front of a screen and also the phone bill can hit the roof.

I think she has a point, don't you? I suppose it's a balance. I still play football and go out with my friends. Staring at a screen all day is not a good idea. But, whichever way you look at it, the Net is definitely here to stay.

Raj Patel

Talking to the reader

Using the work you have already done, complete the two boxes below. Find an example in each paragraph. The first has been done for you in each box.

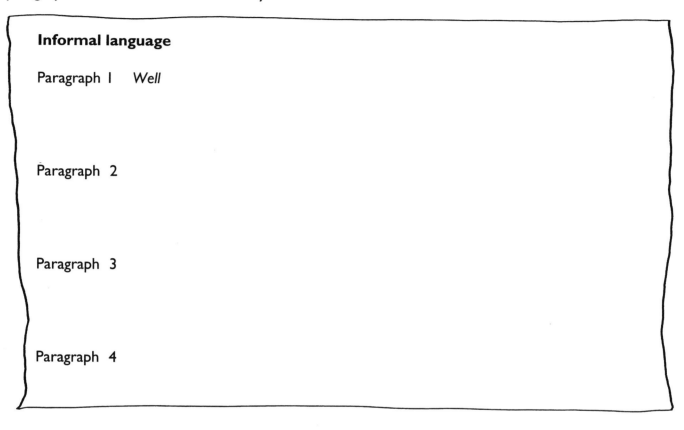

Informal language

Paragraph 1   *Well*

Paragraph 2

Paragraph 3

Paragraph 4

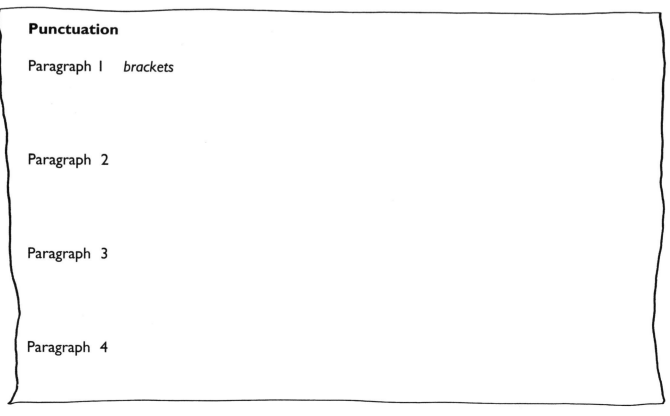

Punctuation

Paragraph 1   *brackets*

Paragraph 2

Paragraph 3

Paragraph 4

Analyse, review, comment

Writing frame

This frame will help you write about your favourite hobby or interest. Refer to the work you have done, such as how to use brackets and dashes. Try to keep your language *informal*.

When I think about it, one of my favourite

It's a favourite with me because

Another point about it is that

It's good for you too, because

Are there any drawbacks? Well

But to finish, I'd like to say that

Analyse, review, comment

Formal and informal analysis II

Personal Commentary

- This unit should be used in conjunction with the previous one, which looks at personal commentary.

Main Objective

- *To explore and use different degrees of formality in written and oral texts.*

Additional Focus

- To identify the writer/reader relationship.

Starter Activity

- In the same way as the previous unit, carry out a brainstorming activity, asking students to give examples of formal types of writing (such as official documents, the wording in bills, a business letter, questionnaires). Discuss the various ways formality can be conveyed through language, which distances the reader from the writer. For example, formal signing off in letters, common phraseology, such as 'where applicable', 'due date' and archaic expressions. Point also to its purpose: to convey authority or importance.

Further Preparation

- Here, students are asked to look at the way in which punctuation and formal language create distance. Like personal commentary, formal analysis is non-chronological, uses the present tense and is evaluative and reflective. However, although not exclusive to formal analysis, comments are usually qualified, reiterated or expanded on. Quotations and footnotes can be used. Punctuation such as quotation marks and semicolons are therefore also used. Read the source material with the students. Discuss its content, clarify meaning, and ask them to describe the tone of the writer's voice, pointing to an example of formal language.

  Having had experience from the previous unit, students can then try to complete the worksheet 'Keeping a distance', page 46, without further help, although they may wish to work in pairs.

  Once completed, ask students to report back. Examples from the text of formal language might be: paragraph 1 'as it is sometimes referred to'; paragraph 2 'this signals'; paragraph 3 'may represent'. Examples of punctuation and references are: paragraph 1 the use of footnotes, paragraph 2 and 3 quotation marks, and the semicolon.

Main Activity/ Using the Frame

- The frame is designed so that a comparison between personal commentary and formal analysis can be made. The students will need to refer to the work done on the previous unit as well as work done here. In tone, the frame is formal itself and students are prompted to give examples to qualify their judgements.

Maximising Attainment

- If useful, discuss the difference between the active and passive tense, noting how the latter creates greater distance (for example, through using the by-phrase). You may wish to point to the following example from the source material: 'It was written by the playwright. The playwright wrote it.' Using the passive also allows personal pronouns and other nouns to be dropped. For example, we could also say, 'It was written around 1606', omitting – but implying – 'by the playwright'. Again, this creates an impersonal style.

Macbeth by William Shakespeare

The Scottish Play, as it is sometimes referred to, was written by the playwright around 1606. It was first performed at court, as far as records tell us. (1)

One of Shakespeare's most infamous villains, Macbeth, was not always so. At the beginning of the play, he is a hero, 'brave Macbeth', a noble soldier returned from battle and rewarded for his loyalty by a grateful king. It is as Thane of Cawdor that Macbeth becomes ambitious; begins to desire the crown and to plot his course of action. This signals disaster. The witches' prophecies prove irresistible and he is drawn further and further towards destruction.

It is a mistake to assume, however, that the 'weird sisters' are responsible for Macbeth's crimes. The witches may represent Fate but Macbeth is driven by his own quest for power too. Similarly, it should not be assumed that Lady Macbeth is responsible. Though she has ambition in excess; to an even greater extent than her husband, she breaks down under the burden of guilt and horror. Macbeth remains fully aware of what he is doing, but he is unable to help himself.

(1) *Shakespeare's Language* Frank Kermode

Keeping a distance

Using the work you have already done, complete the two boxes below. Find an example in each paragraph, which tells you that the writing is formal.

Formal language

Paragraph 1

Paragraph 2

Paragraph 3

Punctuation and references

Paragraph 1

Paragraph 2

Paragraph 3

Analyse, review, comment